T0115089

We Are All Doing
LIFE
Somewhere

Lori Williams and Sandy Schulte

BALBOA.
PRESS

A DIVISION OF HAY HOUSE

ISBN: 978-1-4525-5287-3 (sc)
ISBN: 978-1-4525-5288-0 (e)

Library of Congress Control Number: 2012910023

Balboa Press books may be ordered through booksellers or by contacting:

Balboa Press
A Division of Hay House
1663 Liberty Drive
Bloomington, IN 47403
www.balboapress.com
1-(877) 407-4847

Because of the dynamic nature of the Internet, any web addresses or links contained in this book may have changed since publication and may no longer be valid. The views expressed in this work are solely those of the author and do not necessarily reflect the views of the publisher, and the publisher hereby disclaims any responsibility for them.

The author of this book does not dispense medical advice or prescribe the use of any technique as a form of treatment for physical, emotional, or medical problems without the advice of a physician, either directly or indirectly. The intent of the author is only to offer information of a general nature to help you in your quest for emotional and spiritual well-being. In the event you use any of the information in this book for yourself, which is your constitutional right, the author and the publisher assume no responsibility for your actions.

Any people depicted in stock imagery provided by Thinkstock are models, and such images are being used for illustrative purposes only.
Certain stock imagery © Thinkstock.

Printed in the United States of America

Balboa Press rev. date: 07/17/12

Contents

For as long as I can remember, I have wanted to work in prison. When I was young I saw myself as a helper, healer, teacher, and/ or therapist to the incarcerated, not really knowing what any of that would look like. When I finally got to prison as a budding new psychologist, I still really had no idea what that would look like. I had no idea how my vulnerabilities would be exposed, how I would be humbled again and again, what my passion was, or how I would grow into a better, wiser, more compassionate human being. I had no idea that in this process I would be the teacher and the taught, as well as the healer and the healed. I had no idea that I would "grow up in prison."

This book really is a story about women growing up in prison. As we worked with the women at various times in their incarceration, we noticed that developmental stages occurred based on the nature of the crime, time incarcerated, as well as early developmental issues prior to incarceration. In the initial stages survival and adjustment were paramount while later on issues of 'who am I' and 'what's this all about' came to the forefront. We watched them struggle to negotiate the dilemma of responsibility and self acceptance in spite of their previous actions. We watched them negotiate these issues bravely and courageously in spite of feelings of fear and vulnerability. The poetry illustrates how four women "stared down their demons" in order to become more fully integrated people. I think that the process reflected in the poetry is not unlike what we all go through as we struggle to evolve. After all we are all doing life somewhere.

The project is a result of over 15 years of therapeutic work with the women. For the past year we met weekly to engage in a therapeutic process. The women would take key words from the session that related to one of the categories and write a poem reflective of those ideas. The ideas are outlined in the stages listed below.

Stabilization and Adjustment: 1 to 10 years

Adjustment to long term incarceration is a developmental process, as well as a gradual and overwhelming task. When a woman stares at the possibility of living the rest of her life in prison, she essentially stares into the unknown. The initial years of incarceration require stabilization and adjustment both internally and externally. It is often a period in which the woman feels alienated from herself and others. Everything that was familiar to her becomes foreign.

The very beginning of a prison sentence involves fear of the unknown, especially for women who have not been in prison before. There is the fear of daily life in prison and the stress that prison creates, but on a deeper level there is the threat of loss and disconnection from families and friends who do not know or understand what she is going through. At the same time the inmate does not know what life holds for her. She is focused on struggling to survive, taking care of her basic needs, and learning the unique culture of prison life. For many this time includes feelings of depression and anger, which may be acted out in their daily lives as fights with others and getting disciplinary write ups for defiant behaviors. The inmate often blames her crime on someone else or "the system." She tends to be focused on externalizing her problems and feelings. She resists believing that she is responsible for her situation. The trauma to her identity is profound. Her identity as a person and a mother is shaken, leaving her questioning who she is really.

"I was a hostage to myself and to my past not willing to move forward." ~ Danielle

As the length and reality of her incarceration bears down on her, she experiences a strong sense of loss, hopelessness and despair. She may have been alienated from family, friends, and children, resulting in overwhelming grief. She realizes the loss of her dreams, her potential, a career and the joy of hobbies or traveling. The permanency of these losses becomes paramount. Her life shrinks from infinite possibilities to a very small world of daily prison life. She is still externally focused, believing that these problems are created by some event or entity outside of her control. She continues to place responsibility on things outside of herself.

"I was swimming in a pool of denial." ~ Windy

The potential for stagnation is another part of the Stabilization process. Her life has grown so small that it does not take long to experience all that is available. She does not have many choices of jobs or educational programs to fill her time. There is little variety in her new life. This extends to her social experience. She is stuck with the people around her, including the seven other women with whom she shares a small room. She is not able to walk away when there is conflict in a room. For those with long sentences or life sentences the realization that this is all she has in her life can result in deep despair. This may be all she will have for the rest of her life. She may experience this feeling of stagnation for many years. The loss of hope and the onset of stagnation can result in defiant acting out and self-destructive behavior for those who are angry. As time goes by, she will often experience feeling emotionally fragmented as a person. She will continue to adjust to these difficult feelings.

"At one point I had no hope of getting out of prison. So, I decided to live my life in the world I was in. I would do what I wanted to do." ~ Dani

Developing a deep and meaningful therapeutic process is difficult at this time. Therapy will serve the role of helping her adjust to the environment but will likely not increase the depth of her understanding at this time. The recollections of the crime will come from a shallow point of view based on the denial of the reality of the circumstances that led to her incarceration. The relational stance to the victim is minimal. The shallow understanding of the crime and its impact arises from a sense of disconnection. This disconnection preserves the women's psychic structure in a way that allows her to continue to function. Completely embracing the crime and the impact at this point would further the fragmentation of her fragile self and lead to decompensation. Her defenses will weaken and the therapeutic process will deepen as she shifts into an attitude of accepting more responsibility.

The following poetry is a result of meetings with four women serving life sentences, each of whom have served over 20 years. The poetry corresponds to their stages of development during their incarceration and is divided by themes within those stages which are: Fear, despair, stagnation, choice, hope, integration, and redemption.

FEAR

CHERI

Fear of not fitting in
picked up the first joint
a taste of belonging
was the lime in my tequila
licking the salt off his neck
wasn't I the cool one
Fear
driving me, riding me, owning me
taking me to new and lower levels
looking for the way out of my own skin
Fear of being afraid
picked up the gun
loaded it with the shame
of what I let you do to me
Fear
picked up the empty casings
and pretended I didn't kill you
Fear of myself
picked up the pen
and signed my confession
how cool am I now

DANIELLE

<u>Early 1995</u>

Fear took the drivers seat.
Push, pulse, pull, crack…
then split.
Fragments of self
fallen side by side
worlds apart
Not much alike.
So little action,
emotion filled reaction,
when one equals two.
Disconnect,
distract,
disassociate to hide from the pain –
So much pain I was numb!
I took Jim's advice and broke
on through "to the other side."
Nowhere to go,
no place to run,
no where to hide,
but inside
and it's dark
cold and frozen.
One soft drop away from broken.
She's loving, kind,
when he comes around she's
totally blind
and from behind her eyes
He's watching.

WINDY

The District Attorney said I would
parole while I'm young.
Each day I wake up in a state of
fear
confusion
insecurity
15 to life
What does that mean?
Possibility of paroling while I'm young,
I isolate myself,
Having overwhelming 'why me' feelings,
Can I function in this
reality,
This sure is a long ways away
from Muldrow
Will I be free?
Can I be free?
Is freedom just a word?
Fatigued
Questioning am I still young.

DANI

An Ode to October

In the early morning hours
  before the darkness
        turns to light
I am lost within a delusion
  inside my dreams tonight

Reality is nowhere
  as far as I can see
I hope I will awaken
  before my dreams devour me

I am frightened by the visage
  of the head just floating there
Will I survive this haunting
  or perish from despair?

So real is this horror
  on this October night
When the goblins dance on tombstones
  and the witches
        all take flight

A chilling sound of screaming
  pulls me from this nightmare
Into the light of morning
  and my alarm clock
        ringing there

The memory of my dreaming
  still clings like spider's floss
My heart
  beats running madly
From October's snapping jaws

DESPAIR

DANI

Her eyes are dull
 with despair
Her heart aches with
 longing
For a relationship
 that has grown
        stagnant
His acceptance of the
 change too easy
Her hopes of rebuilding
 dashed
Still she wonders why
 it was her responsibility

DANIELLE

Heart beat
 Broken
Fists pounding on the floor.
I can't take it,
Can't stand it,
I'm far past cracking
Already crossed that line,
Does it count for anything,
Or nothing,
If I pretend the responsibility isn't mine?
Drowning in a muddy river
Of deception and lies
Somebody…
 Anybody…
Throw me a line.
Just one simple word
Or even a hand
A push or a shove
That will help me to stand.
Someone please notice
I'm in way too deep,
I'm an outcast,
A loner,
A monster,
A freak.
If anyone hears me,
Give me a sign
Seems I'm five feet under,
And running out of time.

DANIELLE

I want to cut this out of my life
Out of my heart
Out of my damn mind!!!
Tare myself open to let this all ooze
Out of my rotting body
So I will be no more.
I want to forget it all
Or be able to feel it when I want it
Not this ebb and flow of temporary insanity.
I can not remove myself from who I am
When this happens, please tell me,
I can not be who I've become!
I just am and don't want to be
Blood red emotion
Flowing from my veins
To spill over a world who
Wouldn't notice.

CHERI

What gives me the right to be sane
When it cost you your life?
What kind of Black Magic Voodoo crap
Not to see how twisted I was?
Now I see and I'm forever changed.
Here lies the unacceptable quandary
I took your breath and learned to breath.
If you gave it freely how different I'd feel!
Yet it is the shame of knowing
I wrenched it away from you.
I, a thief of life, waking everyday
You, forever sleeping
Lifting my face to feel the suns warmth,
You, forever cold
I'm saved and condemned
Walking a wire between my own heaven and hell
Seeking balance of who I was and who I am
Accepting that I cannot make this right, ever.

WINDY

Let go of yesterday's tears,
Be grateful I've let them go,
I hold those dried tears with
Gratitude for lessons learned,
Mindful not to repeat the cycle,
Irritated I'm still imprisoned in the belly of
A beast,
A different type of abuser,
Wanting physical freedom,
Needing to start each day new.

WINDY

Most of my life I believed I was
Stagnant in despair,
I accepted my future was a loss of
Hope and no one cared,
I wanted to gain hope and prayed
For a true relationship,
Due to the abuse it seemed I was
To be skipped,
However by taking responsibility
For my life,
Now I have gained hope, acceptance
And receptive to a positive life.

STAGNATION

DANI

Ego, id, the inner child
All of my feelings are neatly filed
My heart beats faint with trepidation
Choices made with expectation
Integration, fabrication, everything's so lame
No help for those who feel not shame

CHERI

Stagnation overwhelms me
Addiction, chaos, insanity
I stink with it
I'm sick with it
I face my despair, it is darkness
Holding the answers I need
I push, but cannot see through it
Yet I yearn for a relationship with myself
And I know it's my responsibility to find me
Amidst the addiction, chaos, insanity
Find the light which is truly me
The hope of my salvation is a fire
Burning through the darkness
Patience, Cheri, Patience
Don't force it, don't push too hard
Acceptance of both darkness and light
Holds the answer, brings the balance
Brings me peace

DANIELLE

Stagnant,
Non-moving,
Frozen Fluidity,
Stuck, Stick in the mud
Concocted, crafted
And filled with despair.
No hope
Living one day at a time…
One day at a time?!
An eternity of empty
Meaningless one days
That fill up the vacant space
That once was my mind,
Broken Relationships,
Broken Dreams,
Broken is Nothing!...
I'm shattered.
Torn, Ripped and Shredded.
Responsibility is a task not
Seen nor taken by this blind woman child.
Acceptance is the dress I wear
And the empty body that wears it is
Stagnant.

WINDY

Loss of all ability to function,
Stagnate
Like a rock growing moss
Depressed
 Cry outburst
Desperate
Hopeless
Stuck on 12/03/1994

Shift to Responsibility: 10 - 20 years

As time progresses a gradual shift to accepting responsibility occurs. She gradually develops an identification with and responsibility for her circumstances as she recognizes that this is indeed about her. She really did play a part in the crime. Then it becomes 'how much of what happened is my fault?' As this is coming more and more into awareness, she may feel despair, anger and impulse to act out. In the beginning the focus remains external. Her thoughts shift from lack of responsibility to 'what do I do to get out of prison?' There is a search for a 'formula' that will make that happen. She focuses on saying and doing the right things to make others happy. She gets involved in educational and self-help activities that she believes will please the Board of Parole Hearing members. When looking back many of the women describe their behavior at that time as "pretending". They were pretending to have a depth of knowledge about what sorts of behaviors led to their incarceration. They do gain some insight during this time, but it tends to be somewhat shallow compared to later therapeutic work. This is a crucial phase that will ultimately allow them to make the shift into genuine responsibility.

> *"I wanted to take responsibility but I did not know what would happen if I did. What would I have? What would I be?"* ~ *Windy*

As time goes on she realizes that she needs to make decisions about her life. She starts to explore her values and starts to make choices based on her current values. For example, escaping the pain of her situation may be replaced with taking steps to face the pain and fight through it. During this time she may become more amenable to psychotherapy and treatment accelerates as she begins to work outside the sessions. She breaks down everything about her life and looks at it from a safe vantage point. She has new thoughts and feelings about the parts. For example, she might realize that her child is the same age as she was when she was abused and she can see her vulnerability as a child for the first time. She sees that she was not responsible for the way adults treated her as a child. These awarenesses are freeing and with that release energy builds to keep on going and clean out all the darkness. It is a process that takes the strength to face her own darkness, to square her shoulders and stare down the demons of her past.

An important moment occurs when she decides to work on herself in more depth; when she chooses to stare down the demons. At that moment she experiences some relief as she realizes that she does have some control over her thoughts and feelings. The focus starts to shift from external blame to internal responsibility. A flicker of hope suggests that she could heal and have a better life.

As this process continues she explores the crime in greater and greater depth; looking at the crime over and over from different angles. Part of the process is looking at how the victim was affected. Her role in the crime becomes clearer. She learns to take responsibility for her role and from that gains more insight. As her insight deepens she gains awareness of the impact of her crime on others. She feels a stronger sense of hope with the empowerment of taking responsibility. She has shifted into taking responsibility but does not yet have complete ownership of her situation. This will come later as all parts of her become deeply integrated.

Discontent about the meaning of her life creates pressure to move beyond this phase.

CHOICE

Dani

Sinking down into
        awareness
holding my breath
        diving deep

Watching for the demons
  who guard my memories
        in the dark

Emotions swim here
        with purpose
  Flashing silver
        quick and sure

Rising unasked to
        the surface
  Seeking the light
        and warping the façade
  with ripples

CHERI

How long have I slept, unknowing and unknown
Walking through dreamscapes, believing in shadows
Disconnected from truth, faith in the lie
I awaken, looking back upon the path I've traveled
Littered with the wreckage of broken hearts and shattered
lives
I scream to the universe, to God, to anyone who
May have pity, I'm sorry,
But sorry is just what I've become
So I must stay awake and make a choice
head in a new direction, leave myself open,
Vulnerable as a child and learn to walk again
A babe in old clothes and an older heart
Healing and renewing as the miles pass
And amends are made, then it's up to me
To wake up the next one.

CHERI

Just for today, be mindful
Live this day with gratitude
Always aware of the difference
Between needs and wants
Letting go of frivolous things
So I may hold more tightly
Things of the heart
Happiness is my frame of mind
I create it by what I choose
I want less irritation, so I want less
Right here, right now, all is well

CHERI

One night I dreamt, or was I awake?
Perhaps a vision
I rose above my bunk, roof, then sky
Lifted and then pulled into space
incredible, magnificent
I could sense the speed with my soul
though I felt no wind, heard no sound
My own thoughts and some kind of knowing
served as the voice of my guide
Exhilaration to be going upward,
surprise really
a profound sense of gratitude, relief, and happiness
overwhelmed me, humbled me, freed me of condemnation.
In my excitement I chanced a glance,
to see my world from the lofty vantage of angels and
astronauts
but alas, I was not allowed
for death does not look back
So I looked up with expectation,
only to face an endless, rolling wall of fire
The only way forward was through it
Enter with faith of a child
For isn't such the Kingdom of God?
I froze with fear, knowing the chaff
that would burn away would be me
Indecision brings me back to my cell
Next time I choose the fire.

CHERI

I surrender my inalienable rights as a human being
To be selfish, ignorant, prejudice, unseeing
To carry on the hatred, fear, small-mindedness and
Wastefulness of my forefathers.

I surrender to Grace, the intangible mentor
Whom under her tutelage changes my perception
Of this world I find myself in,
This world molded by ones who came before me.

I am but one, but I am one of many
Who rather than look behind at past mistakes
Look ahead though eyes of faith and vision
Awakened to the truth that we are one.

We pay attention, stay mindful, focus
Our intentions to the betterment of the species,
To the wellbeing of our home, our earth
Care about what we do to ourselves and each other.

Our source is love, and love is generous
It gives us what our hearts desire
So let us keep vigil over our hearts and minds
So we may leave a lighter foot print,
For our children to follow.

DANIELLE

Sit
Silence
Pin drop
Drop of water in the bucket
Wait...inhale...
Breath.
Mindful of this moment,
Oh to be in this very moment,
And each that follows.
Let go,
Disconnect
From hopes, expectations and memories.
Just be.
Separate needs from wants
Learn to only want what I need
And nothing more –
Don't settle for anything less.
Gratitude fills my heart,
Fills my lungs as I pull in air,
Breath.
First breath of life
Taken a million times over
As I am reborn each second of each day,
For each moment is new.
Pause.
Breath.
Just sit
Be with that irritating itch
I want to scratch just behind my eyes.

DANIELLE

I decided to pay attention
Learn each lesson
With grace.
I surrendered to my powerlessness
To become empowered
And admitted I was wrong
For the thousandth time again.
I stopped sitting around
Waiting for the pain to end.
I stood up on my own two feet
And then,
I made that first step in faith
Gave up saving face,
Made the choice to trust myself
But wait…
I changed my perception
Changed my direction
Turned around and leapt
Into the great abyss.
A life that once looked cold, dark and hard
Turned out to be a warm, light loving friend.

WINDY

Nobody wants to be vulnerable
Affected by
Words
Actions
Baggage
 Triggers
Drowning in a sea of vulnerability.
Am I way too exposed
Do I believe in what I feel?
Like a thousand insects,
Crawling in an open wound
Closed
Not wearing my heart on my sleeve
I put my poker face on
Is that the way life is supposed to be?
Or is it like a butterfly,
Each day raising out of it's cocoon
Being vulnerable to the great adventures,
Knowing how to love
Isn't it lovely,
Isn't it the way life is supposed to be?

WINDY

I couldn't find laughter in the darkness,
Chained to the demons of my past,
First I had to admit that a façade was my life,
Lesson learned through accountability,
Emotions once lost, now found,
Surrendering the resistance I found awareness in healing,
Choosing to let go of the demon of my past
I embrace lightness like an angel kiss
My world now is a healing bliss.

WINDY

Stepp'n out to find independence,
Wanting to make the right choices,
I stopped competing with the demons of my past,
In order to start a new,
I must have a clean slate,
Slowly I let go,
Scared and frightened of taking the wrong
Direction,
Slowly I let go,
In some of my darkest and painful hours,
I kept believing that the universe would send
Me "u mail" to guide me,
And I would begin to care and love myself,
Finally, I took responsibility of self,
And was awaken to a beautiful vulnerable place,
Of a woman who is perfect,
Perfect without baggage of the past.
I have the faith that every experience
Has been for a reason,
I believe with grace I am always perfect
For where I am in life.

HOPE

DANI

Be mindful of your manners
Be mindful of the traffic
So many things to remember
My head is a mind fill
teeming with the leftovers
of so many people's lies
and truths and spools
of good advice
Questions without answers
stories with no end
lying at the bottom
My mind is filled to overflowing
packed full with the rubble
of my wanting, and the
worry, and the needing
So slip into the mix
but be mindful
of the irritation
you will find
In the passage
coarse with the salt
From the tears upon tears
of grief and pain and madness
So search for the door
the hatch the exit
and take with you the good,
the true, the wise
Let go of the refuse
let go the confusion

Let it fly
with gratitude and a sigh
and watch it travel
Forever
into nowhere

Dani

I've been living on the
other side of reason
Receiving fragments of madness
from someone who went
postal a long time ago

But lately I've been wondering
What would happen if
I pushed
against the wall of preservation
would I meet myself
on the other side of fear?

And what would be the reaction?
A quaking in the granite?
A splitting of the psyche?
Or nothing?
Nothing at all?

I still receive the messages
From the calls that
go unanswered
And still I wonder
what would happen
If I met myself on
the other side of hell?

CHERI

Delusions of grandeur was the safety blanket
Of a frightened child in a woman's façade
The subconscious quest to survive creating
a caricature of the true self, trapped
within a web of infinite deceits,
reality lost in the dream, the dream
turning into the despair of living a lie
she awakens to truth and with it a hope
sanity becomes tangible, reachable,
acceptance of what was and what is
merges into a pathway of peace.

DANIELLE

The universe calls out unbidden
And grants my desires
At the price of faith.
I must be vulnerable,
Believe in that which I can not see.
Face the direction of the rising sun
Unblinkingly stare in the face of purity.
Awaken to a new reality
One decorated with fairies, sprites,
Trolls, gnomes, dragons and mer-folk.
Catch a shooting star, ride on a moon beam
Astrally dance among the clouds.
Consciously,
Make a choice to live in magick and mystery,
Remembering,
Endless possibility resides right here
Inside of me.

DANIELLE

Swimming up
from the funneling tear filled
whirl pool of despair
nearly drowned,
I was flailing
and gasping for air.
Not enough,
couldn't quite fill my lungs.
I could not seem to break away,
detach,
From where I came from.
Death of much of my old self,
rebirth into new life,
transformation of a moth,
changed into butterfly.
Redeemed from my past,
built on coffee stained lies.
Comfort in the future
knowing that this day,
the present,
is mine.

DANIELLE

Light chases away the demon filled darkness
And soothes my hardened soul.
Emotions run freely
to wash clean the façade
that once gave me comfort
much like, for some, does a home.
Awareness is high,
a new purpose come 'round,
each day, a new day,
my true self is found.

WINDY

In life's dance we experience it all,
We live, laugh and love,
We experience loss and despair
At it's greatest depths,
Yet in the death from
The loss and despair there is a
Rebirth of a comfort,
Redemption as we hope
Like a phoenix tearfully
Rises from its ashes,
With hope
And we dance experiencing
A new song.

WINDY

Expectation of what I wanted others to do
Always let me down
Submerged in ego
Along with it came shame
What a destructive game,
Breaking down I came to a realization
Let it all go
The integration of healthy choices
Spoke by my own voice
Finding the balance of love, self, and ego
Wow look at me go.

Existential Life Issues: 20+ years

During this time existential life issues, such as purpose and meaning, become the focus of exploration. Piece by piece our inmate identifies the dysfunction of her life before incarceration; may times expressing relief at not living like that anymore. She has a strong belief that she would "never go there again", never have the same behaviors and beliefs. In the same turn she knows that she cannot fix the results of the crime. She now becomes internally focused on what she can change. She engages in activities that provide enrichment and clarification of her internal growth and values. Activities that were done for external reasons, such as to please the parole board, fall by the way side. She realizes how much she was pretending to change and actively pushes herself further into her darkness and craves more depth of knowledge and understanding. She has to learn to forgive herself and others. When she can do this she is able to accept her situation and accept herself.

A deeper understanding of the crime is gained from this work. A sense of empathy for all those impacted is achieved, resulting in a more full sense of responsibility. Embracing responsibility is a catalyst toward meaning and hope.

Integration of the self involves deep exploration of the inner self particularly those parts that are hidden. According to Freudians, integration becomes possible through bringing unconscious motivation into conscious awareness. Jungian's discuss integration through exploring the shadow side of the personality and bringing those shadow qualities into the light. Theory aside, integration of the self involves deep personal exploration and a willingness to look honestly and courageously into the deepest part of yourself into those places that hold your deepest fear, your deepest shame, as well as your deepest vulnerability. I like to refer to the process as "staring down your demons." For female lifers the question of integration involves a molding of dichotomies such as "How can I be a person who cares deeply, loves my family and friends, cares about the welfare of others and simultaneously be a person who took the life of another?" In other words how do I embrace polar opposites: light and dark, life and death, good and evil?

These questions cannot adequately be answered by intellectual experience if integration is to occur, they must be answered at an internal experiential level.

Integration is important because that which you cannot face "owns you". Lacking integration she goes through life avoiding and tip toeing around her fears rather than living fully in the moment. She walks around waiting for "the other shoe to drop" wondering what people are thinking of her, hoping that they never find out who she really is. She feels ingenuous, but fights to maintain her façade. To live fully and freely in the moment she must integrate the totality of her experience.

> *"The demons you face can no longer haunt you."*
> *~Windy*

The process of integration is a lengthy developmental process and does not occur over night. Each stage of development that she faces during incarceration is significant as she approaches integration. Denial, despair and fear have all been part of the process that leads her to owning herself completely. She finds meaning in what once seemed meaningless and hope where none previously existed. The hope is no longer specific to release from the physical prison where she has lived for so many years, but hope of escaping the internal chains that have kept her bound for all this time. She's no longer self involved, and seeks to find ways to make amends for past mistakes. She looks at ways to further explore her own redemption by seeking ways to give back to others.

At this point she seeks ways to change for the better, to repay society and shed debt. Her focus is on what she can do for others as a form of redemption and rebirth. She can become someone completely new through the healing process of finding ways to make up for the pain she has caused. Of course, nothing seems a sufficient payment, however, any steps toward redemption is working in the right direction. When you are not intentionally causing pain to others and putting energy toward helping others you are doing the work of redemption.

Altruism is the best answer to despair, stagnation, and fear. It is making connections with others and improving things in their life that leads to personal growth. Some inmates go to self-help activities and just go through the motions. There is a significant difference between that and actually growing and healing from these activities. There is a noticeable difference in the inmate when she makes this change, such as being less tense, and is able to access the depths of her person and fight off the demons of guilt and shame. Altruism many times goes hand-in-hand with social interaction. Now she is communicating with the outside world (outside herself). From this social interaction friends are made and peer support is built.

The contemplation of existential issues often results from the process at this point. She makes some decisions about what is important to her. She may choose to continue with some of her activities while letting others stop. She realizes that she is gaining a sense of purpose and meaning in the activities she chooses as her own. This may also fit with a spiritual path she is walking resulting in more meaning and structure for her life.

INTEGRATION

DANI

Am I okay in my truth?
 Is the integration of guarded
          omissions
 with the healing of raw honesty
          enough?
Will I receive an honorable mention
 in the competition of life?
Patience belongs to a virtuous woman
 her eyes full of wisdom
peace flowing from her
                    like contentment
This is the woman I want to become
 loving and affectionate
Perhaps after forgiveness
 and understanding
Removes the stain of guilt
So I watch the skies for Judgment Day
 where I will kneel at the feet of
                    perfection

CHERI

For judgments I have no affection
They bring no peace, no healing
Just superiority, condemnation
Humiliations, punishment, fear
How can fear live with love?
For love is the source of creation
In it is humility, wisdom, patience
Humility does not judge, but it learns
From experiences, and with patience
It nurtures growth, and then awakening comes
And we remember who we truly are.
It is my responsibility to honor my truth
And accept things for what they are.
We punish one another for being human,
Yet is it not why we are here?
Divinity travels with me, ever the watcher
It is my source and strength, my fellow traveler
Through this material plane.
There are no judgments or condemnation
From divinity. God is not concerned with
Our petty imaginings. Life is the adventure
Of being human, the good and the bad of
It is part of the journey. In the end
We integrate into the one source from
Which we came, so stop judging and
start loving.

DANIELLE

The shame of poorly made choices
Threatened to engulf me
When I realized for the umpteenth time
I had made another poor choice in you
And in you and you and you
And each and every one of you before and after you.
Each time left feeling let down,
Battered, torn apart and confused.
I learned from the best of you
That big expectations lead to big disappointments
So I decided to expect nothing at all.
I asked nothing and received a
Million dollars worth of absolutely nothing!
Each day I watched as you served your
Pathetic little ego that no one but you
Cared a thing about,
I lived in my Id brain,
Survival, primitive and primal
Never dreaming of the land of mid or beyond,
A way to break out.
Today I live in a sea of serenity
Having integrated the many selves
I was once shattered into being.
Free of all broken promises, insecurities and lies,
Able to see me without disguise.
Living and loving a world of my own
I've finally discovered, found,
The path I have chosen

DANIELLE

Will all hope be lost
As I watch reality bunny hop
Across that open field?
Will delusional fear filled fantasies
Become my insanity
As despair fills my crumpled body
Now marionette strings cut and fallen to the floor?
Will the pendulum swing
As survival kicks in
Because the past and the present
Are merging?

CHERI

Life may seem a charade
Yet there lies a purpose in the journey
The quest of the soul to find its essence, its source
Souls searching within the play of reality
The grand stage with all its players and their bit parts
Drama, comedy, tragedy, suspense,
How we cheer for the hero and hiss the villain!
Only to grasp in the final scene
An awareness of the underlying truth
That angels of light and demons of darkness
Both have the starring roles, equally important,
Necessary to the plot, creating the whole
The concept of good vs. evil is life's storyline
Making it, exciting, dangerous, mysterious
Challenging us to play our best at the part we've been given
The Director skillfully balancing the light and dark
Because at the end of the story, we, all of us
Hold hands together to take our final bows
And as the curtain falls, leave as one cast.

WINDY

Hey you, Lil' Baby, it was all about me as I
Walked the yard with a smile,
Yet under the mask I wore in my silence –
I was scared, frightened in this new reality
Called prison.
I was lost, wishing I could click my heels 3
Times and be at home, even in it's dysfunction
The thoughts I welcomed
Despair clung to me like the drab state issue
Clothing.
I made a choice throw the negative away like
The past
Hope floats, choice made, ready to merge back
Into an unfamiliar society, healed.
It is all about me.

WINDY

Integration into a foreign community. PRISON!
Judgments from Society has left an emotional
Scar.

In becoming okay in my truth, I have learned
  Humility, honor, wisdom, and patience.

Accepting responsibility.......I can love myself now,

Show a deep affection for self and appreciate the distance
in my
  Journey I am traveling.

I watch others in their healing journey,

I greet them each day with an open heart.

REDEMPTION

DANI

It is the winter of my life
  and redemption is a
          treasure worth chasing
For it wasn't so long ago
  that comfort was found
          in the arms of sleep
  and despair would greet
          me when I woke
But just as the Seasons
  cycle on and on
          and the death of the sun
  only heralds its rebirth
So it is that the ups
          and downs
  are the heartbeat
          of living

CHERI

The little girl is soft, pliable
Eager to be molded into the likeness
Of her heroes
Her role models are unaware of their power
Power to create outside the womb
Demanding and short sighted
Their expectations are unrealistic
For they are but babes themselves
Their choices create her path
Shame, fear, confusion, anger
Constant companions that eventually
Integrate into her ego, her line
Of defense, and eventually her downfall
Now on her own path, she sheds the
Accumulation of other people's baggage
She re-invents herself and becomes herself
Freedom!

CHERI

The darkness I feared
Has shown itself a friend
Hiding the shame until
I'm strong enough to accept truth
It holds me gently
Like a womb, safe and quiet
Re-birth is the promise of enlightenment
But first there is pain, fear, revelations
Then the breath of life, redemption
But the cord is not cut from darkness
It comes with me to keep the deep place safe
While I grow strong, grow up, search it out
Then it will visit again to take me deeper still.
I find my comfort now in times of despair
For I know it foreshadows death
Death of old imprints upon my soul
Survival tactics no longer necessary
So that my heart opens a little more
Letting the light in, letting life in.

DANIELLE

Rewind to
Judgment,
Condemnation,
Shoved down my throat responsibility
Unwanted shame,
Painted on by blame,
Unforgiving
No where to turn,
No place to run,
A bug burnt under your giant magnifying glass.
I am small,
Insignificant,
Invisible,
Until you catch me in your peripheral
To scorn me.
Fast forward 16 years,
Integration for past to present
On a journey
A mission
Of healing
I dine of the feast of my truth
As I trudge on with hope,
Patience,
Grateful for change,
I am honored.
This is not a spectator sport
Don't watch or wait idly on the sideline
With these words I warn you.
I dove into the frozen lake,
And warmed by the love,
Peace in my heart,
The iced piece of my heart is thawing.

No longer fooled by false wisdom
False pride
I am humbled.
Affected by time
Moving forward in life
I have found me.

WINDY

18 years picking up the soul of one, once scattered,
Thank God I am free at last,
Free at last free at last who gives a damn
About the past,
No more split psyche,
I have found the internal key,
I'm okay with me,
My reactions once border insanity
Split and torn my emotions were
I've stared down the demons and hope has
Carried to the other side,
Today I am free at last free at last
Thank God I am free and not giving
A damn about the past.

Windy

Through faith and by grace alone I have found peace,
Surrendering to self comes easily,
A choice I once wrestled with,
Now is a chosen path,
Perceptions of mine have changed,
I pay attention to my heart,
I ask, believe and receive
All that my heart desires
I accept it all with warm graceful smiles.

Biographies
Cheri

I believe I was unconscious long before I became an addict and a killer. The absolute insanity and selfishness of the lifestyle that ultimately brought me here never ceases to amaze and terrify me. The saying "when you know better, you do better" is the truth of my journey, and the knowing better began in the form of a spiritual awakening in 1998. Literally being new-born, I have been growing and learning everyday. The life I live now, the person I am today is the most normal, natural, and rewarding state of being I have ever experienced. It's like I've awakened to who I was meant to be all along.

Attempting to transmit the grief, gratitude and grace that has carried me through this journey. I hope some one may be able to touch upon that part of themselves to identify the common threads that hold us all.

> Fear of not fitting in
> picked up the first joint
> a taste of belonging
> was the lime in my tequila
> licking the salt off his neck
> wasn't I the cool one
> Fear
> driving me, riding me, owning me
> taking me to new and lower levels

looking for the way out of my own skin
Fear of being afraid
picked up the gun
loaded it with the shame
of what I let you do to me
Fear
picked up the empty casings
and pretended I didn't kill you
Fear of myself
picked up the pen
and signed my confession
how cool am I now

Windy

California is the place to be, that was what was told to me. My graduation present was a one-way ticket to California. A southern girl in a big city with no coping skills.

Victimized by family, I went out to find my own protection. It was an environment I was used to – dysfunctional and unhealthy. The more I hated myself the worse he treated me.

Prison was the end result of the relationship. Denial was my life ... I denied anything and everything ... blaming came along with the denial. I blamed everyone for my imprisonment and feelings of helplessness. I lived under a heavy cloud of guilt. Stagnate in my own despair. I wanted something different.

Through guidance, I have now accepted who I am today. Taking responsibility for my life is the best thing anyone could have given me. I have stepped out of my self imposed prison and I am free.

Overwhelmed,
Anxious
I can't breathe,
I'm going where?
Prison?
I can't move,
high hopes,

crumbling down,
I should had known
Me, a murderer?
This can't be,
Who am I?
W62147?
Validating I am nobody,
I am the victim,
I lost everything
Oh, why didn't I die
How long can I live this way?
Months,
Years,
Decades,
I can't face the truth,
My own façade,
Full of despair,
Stagnate in hopelessness,
chained,
submerged by my ego,
Surrender the resistance,
Stared down the demons,
Accountable for my actions,
Accepting responsibility,
I am free.

Dani

I was arrested for murder when I was 22. Although some people believe we are of a responsible age at 21. I think it's debatable.

I am 55 today. The lessons I've learned in prison could never be duplicated in the free world.

However, I do know that we can and do create our own prisons without having to break any laws. In these situations, maybe we are living parallel lives.

My own experiences were intense, but after moving through them I am so much stronger here on the other side of them.

All of my emotions feel the same inside or outside the walls. Depression, love, joy, sorrow, guilt or pride, all these things help us mature.

Drs. Williams and Schulte were both instrumental in my growth being guides and helping me navigate the tangle of my feelings.

I am grateful they were there when I finally faced my demons.

Evolving

Fingers pointing, whispers hidden
Behind smiles that slip as I pass
On their faces hatred is written
My fear is transparent as glass

If I look down at the ground they can't see me.

I play this game everyday
Look at the grass it's so pretty
Talking out loud all the way

At night the despair rushes darkly
Chasing all of the pretense away
Madness stands out starkly
My God, where are you I pray

In time you survive or surrender
You either make do or you don't
Soon only a few will remember
Things that you can't or you won't

Oblivion had become my best friend
Folding me sweetly in dream
No more did the madness descend
Together we were more than we seemed

But truth refused to stay under

The past would not leave me alone
Now comes the rain and the thunder
The storm I must face on my own

Choose to go back or forward instead
Hoping forgiveness will come
A journey starts with one step it is said
And my journey may never be done

Am I worthy of redemption
Am I humble enough today
To explain it was not my intention
To take someone's life away?

Danielle

16 ½ years ago I would have never guessed I would be where I am today. I am not talking about this physical prison. Prison was a distant possibility, jail more than likely, drug addicted, sure. Mental institutions, probably. Death before I was 31, definitely. None of that really mattered back then though. I was in a prison of mental bars and emotional scars that made the future seem irrelevant. My life, and that of most others, really seemed insignificant. So what I meant when I said, "I would have never guessed I would be where I am today" is that I am free. I am free of limiting belief systems, negative thinking patterns and low self esteem. I am free of the bondage I was placed in by my abusers and through compassionate self forgiveness and self love I am free of the bondage of guilt, unforgiveness and shame I'd locked myself in. Today I judge myself to be successful. I believe in the power that I possess as a divine human being. I am a loving, kind, empathetic, trustworthy, forgiving woman who is worthy of positive experiences. I humbly acknowledge my many wrong doings without judgment and condemnation. I know I've taken so much from this world and strive each day to give just a little back as a friend, positive role model, drug and alcohol counselor, mentor, facilitator and an advocate for healing and personal growth.

Fear filled memory,
Very first memory,

Each one built on the other
To create my castle of lies.
I lived in a tower of despair,
Alone, isolated, empty,
Calling out, there's no one there.
Dredging through a mile of quicksand,
With lead for legs and feet
I'm fighting and running;
There is no one to beat.
I became stagnant, unmoving,
Not growing at all.
Pushing and pulling,
I stood,
Just to
  Fall.
I was ready to give up,
To throw in the towel,
Talk about finding grace
At the very last hour.
I chose to start living,
To stop pretending I'd died.
To throw off my armor
And stop building the lie.
I wasn't the victim,
Not on that night,
How dare I,
How could I,
Who gave me the right?
With painful acceptance,
I lifted my head,
To gaze in the distance
Though my heart filled with dread.
No hope filled strike of lighting,
Nor instantaneous flash,

But lit just a glimmer
In the palm of my hand.
Soon I grew to stop hating
The person I'd been,
To stop being her punisher
And start being her friend.
Guide her with compassion
And love in my heart,
To lead her gently,
Out of the dark.
I integrated past and present
Utilized the golden key
I embraced the girl I had been
 And believed in the woman I could be.
With hard work and determination,
I could finally see,
The forgiveness I was seeking,
Residing within me.
Prison wall do not hold me,
No longer hostage to my past,
Made changes and healing,
The kind that will last.
Redemption not found,
In being set free,
But in loving and being,
The best version of me.